BOdies

Philip Ardagh

illustrated by **Mike Gordon**

SCHOLASTIC

For Freddie, of course!

P.A.

Consultant: Dr Hilary Richards,
Faculty of Life Sciences, UCL.

Editorial Director: Lisa Edwards
Senior Editor: Jill Sawyer

Scholastic Children's Books,
Euston House, 24 Eversholt Street,
London NW1 1DB, UK
a division of Scholastic Ltd
London ~ New York ~ Toronto ~ Sydney ~ Auckland
Mexico City ~ New Delhi ~ Hong Kong

First published in the UK by Scholastic Ltd, 2009

ISBN 978 1407 10717 2

Printed and bound by Tien Wah Press Pte. Ltd, Singapore

10 9 8 7 6 5 4 3 2 1

Philip Ardagh and Mike Gordon are regular visitors to Henry's House. Philip (the one with the beard) keeps a note of everything that's going on, and even reads a mind or two. Mike (the one without the beard) sketches whatever he sees, however fantastical it may be ... and together they bring you the adventures of Henry, an ordinary boy in an extraordinary house!

Contents

Welcome to Henry's House!

The human skeleton

Jaggers?

Yes?

Why is there a huge skeleton lying on the floor?

Perhaps he's tired.

The smallest bone in the human body is the stirrup. We have one in each ear.

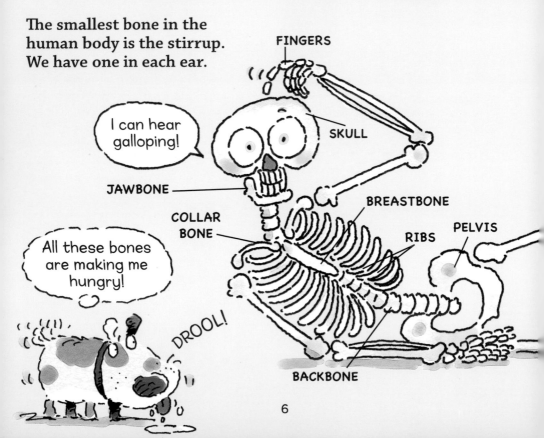

I can hear galloping!

All these bones are making me hungry!

DROOL!

FINGERS

SKULL

JAWBONE

COLLAR BONE

BREASTBONE

RIBS

PELVIS

BACKBONE

6

The longest bone in the human body is the thigh bone.

THIGH BONE

KNEECAP

SHIN BONE

TOES

ANKLE BONES

7

Dr Ray's bony facts

As we grow older, some smaller bones join together to make bigger ones.

Babies are born with around 350 bones. When they are fully grown they only have 206.

Don't look at me!

My skeleton is on the outside of my body!

Bones are hard on the outside...

...and a bit spongy on the inside.

The spongy bit is called marrow.

(Bones are three-quarters made of water.)

A BUG

Along with animals such as gorillas, we humans have opposable thumbs.

This means that we can touch the tips of our thumbs to the tips of all our fingers on the same hand.

This makes us brilliant at using tools or playing the piano.

I can't play the piano. I'm not very musical.

?????!

GRRRR!

Muscles are what get us moving, lifting, running, jumping, even sitting.

Our most powerful muscles are on the sides of our mouth. They're just right for biting!

Muscles can pull but not push.

Muscles are usually fixed to our bones by a kind of strong string called tendons.

TENDONS

These muscles are bending the arm up by pulling the bone.

BONE

When these muscles pull the bone, the arm will straighten.

Skin underfoot

Your skin keeps your insides IN and the outside OUT.

It covers your body with a waterproof oil.

Your skin pumps out salty water, called sweat, to cool you down.

Touch sensors in your skin help you tell rough things from smooth ones.

EPIDERMIS DERMIS

Pain sensors make you feel pain when your skin is hurt.

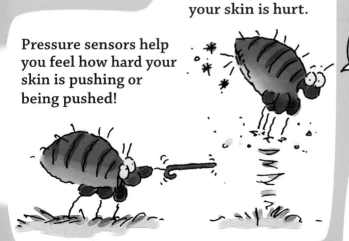

Pressure sensors help you feel how hard your skin is pushing or being pushed!

OUCH!

And you can guess what heat sensors do!

Heaven nose!

By the way…

It's impossible to sneeze with your eyes open.

Our nose makes between one and two PINTS (up to a litre) of mucus a day!!!

I wish dogs could carry umbrellas!

ATISHOO!

AAAAAAGH!

The average sneeze shoots out at an amazing 100 miles an hour (160 kph)!

Drool! Slurp!

Some scientists don't think that umami (a savoury kind of taste) is really its own separate taste type.

18

Have a look at your face in the bottom of this saucepan, Henry, and stick out your tongue.

If you insist!

Our tongues are covered in sensors called tastebuds.

Your spit helps you to taste your food as well as making it easier to swallow.

Parts of the tongue pick up some flavours more easily than others.

Sweet things taste sweetest when put on the tip of the tongue.

The way food smells and feels affects the way it tastes.

A breath of fresh air

Air comes in through our nose and mouth.

It passes down our windpipe into our lungs.

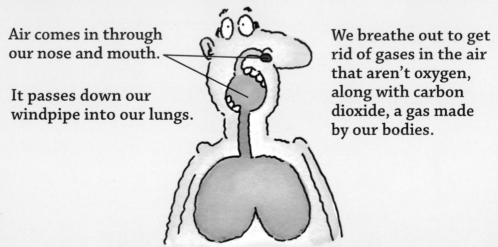

We breathe out to get rid of gases in the air that aren't oxygen, along with carbon dioxide, a gas made by our bodies.

If we didn't breathe out, we'd blow up like balloons!

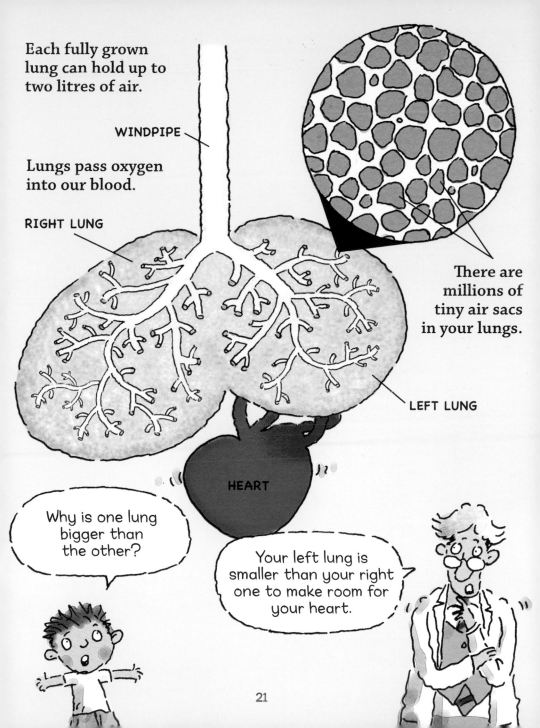

The heart is a large muscle. It pumps blood around the body.

The average heart beats about 100,000 times a day. That's over 36 million times a year!

Without a heart to pump it, our blood would not flow.

Women's hearts beat faster than men's.

An adult human heart can build up enough pressure to squirt blood up to 10 metres. SQUI
RTSQQU IRTSS SSSSSSSSS SSSSS
SQQURTTTS QQQQQQ QQQQQQQ
QQRTTT TFP TZSTUIGI BIFXBWFZ
ZBXWWW ghdvsjhdhdf djhdfgjkshf
jfhfkjfh kf jfkfsksrurf
jhfs….>>>>>>::&%^$%$£%^

SPLUTTER!
KERCHUNK!
PHUT! PHUT!
PHUT!
FIZZ!
BANG!

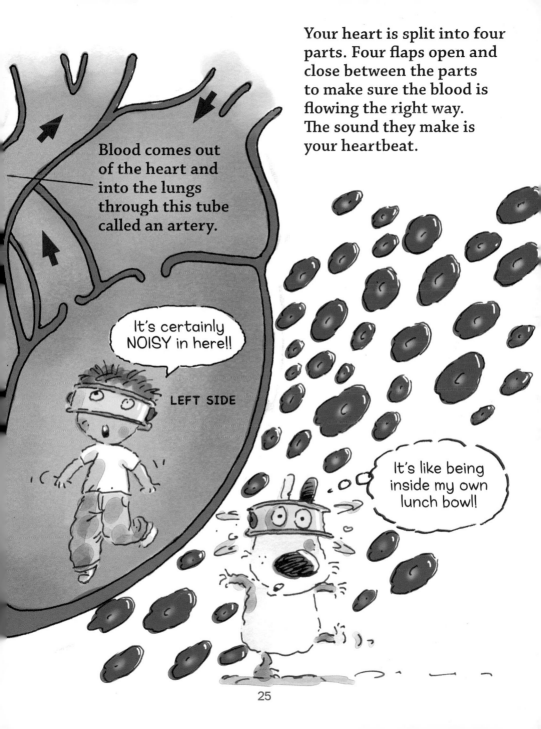

The blood! The blood!

Magnus Boffin's visors are incredible!

Some of his inventions work much better than others! He is very clever, though.

Could he tell us why some bruises turn black and blue - like this old one on my arm?

We need to nip down to the cellar and drop in on the Bates family - the house's resident blood experts.

HI GUYS, HOW'S IT HANGING?

Our resident blood experts are VAMPIRE BATS?

Human blood contains red blood cells, white blood cells and platelets.

RED BLOOD CELL

PLATELETS

WHITE BLOOD CELL

There are around 250 million red blood cells in a drop of blood, along with 13 million platelets and 375,000 white blood cells.

Red blood cells carry oxygen around the body.

They look a bit like doughnuts. Would you like one?

Er – blerch! No thanks. I'm not hungry!

White blood cells are like soldiers in an army, defending our bodies against tiny invaders called germs.

ATTACK!!!

WHITE BLOOD CELL

Excuse me! You're not getting through without the password!

Not everyone's blood is the same. There are four types of blood – A, B, AB and O.

Sorry! I don't know how that tomato ketchup got in there!

Two million new red blood cells are made EVERY SECOND. And they last for about 120 days.

But what is a bruise?

If your body is hit, blood from broken blood vessels sometimes leaks out under the surface of your skin. This is a bruise. As the blood loses oxygen, the bruise goes from red to purple, black or even yellow.

What have we ear?

Those bats have such squeaky voices, they're making my ears ring!

Actually, that's my mobile... Hello?... Hello?

And how DO ears work, anyway?

A trip to here, the Whispering Staircase, might help explain.

Like a number of the strange things in this house, Henry, it was built by your great-great-grandfather.

The entrance is like the sticky-out part of your ear, designed to catch sounds.

HELP! It's not as easy as it looks.

YERCH! Someone carved those statues of famous composers out of earwax!

Earwax helps protect your ears but TOO MUCH earwax can stop you hearing properly.

BALANCING ACT

Inside your ears there are tiny tubes filled with liquid.

As you move around, the liquid moves around too, bending special tiny hairs.

The hairs send messages to your brain. They tell it what way you move, to help you keep your balance.

This part of the ear sends sound signals to the brain.

Nerves send the signals to the brain.

Something to shout about!

The windipe carries air to your lungs.

LUNGS

The voice box is the part of the throat used for speaking.

To speak, shout, laugh or sing, air from your lungs is blown past two thick bands in your voice box.

The air makes the bands wobble, creating a sound. The bands are short and tight when you make a high sound.

The bands are longer and looser when you make a low sound.

By changing the shape of your mouth...

...and moving your tongue and lips...

...you can change the sounds once they've left your voice box.

If I play dead, will she stop making those frightening faces?

BURP!

Oops!

People burp about fifteen times a day. It's just unwanted gas – air – escaping through our mouths!

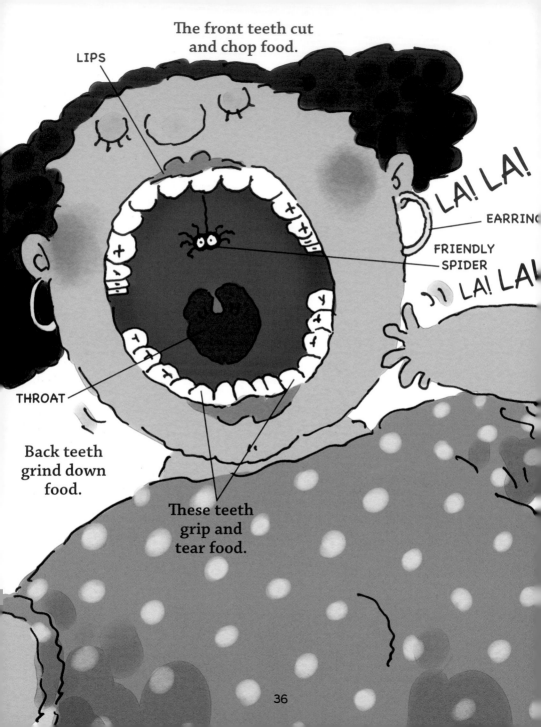

The front teeth cut
and chop food.

LIPS

LA! LA!

EARRING

FRIENDLY
SPIDER

LA! LA!

THROAT

Back teeth
grind down
food.

These teeth
grip and
tear food.

Hard to swallow

Oh, it's you two again...

THREE. Can't you count?

I was wondering what happens to our food once our teeth have chomped it.

More foodie questions. Great! When you eat, your tongue rolls your food into small mushy balls.

These balls are forced into the tube that leads to your stomach and you swallow them down.

Bands of muscles squeeze the food along. You could even eat standing on your head.

Which must be useful if you're a bat...

Stop looking at me like that, Mothball!!

Once you've swallowed, food takes up to three days to travel through lots of tubes...

...A grown-up's digestive system is about 9 METRES long!!!

This lovely "MR FOOD" tea towel will help me to explain.

MR FOOD'S INCREDIBLE JOURNEY

1. First, Mr Food travels from your mouth to your stomach.

STOMACH

2. In your stomach, Mr Food is squeezed and mixed with special juices ... turning him into a thick mush. The liver makes juices to help digest Mr Food.

100% IRISH LINEN

3. Next, Mr Food passes into a tube called your small intestine. Here, useful chemicals are taken out of him and sent around your body.

KIDNEYS

4. The large intestine soaks up water and sends it to your kidneys.

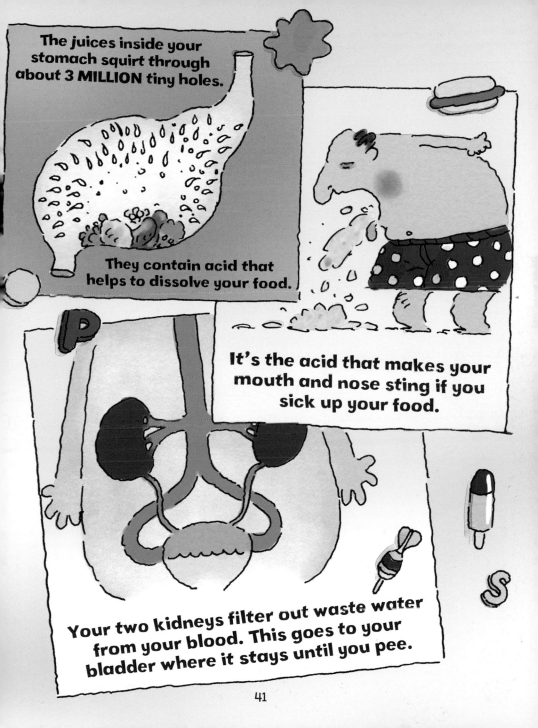

The juices inside your stomach squirt through about 3 **MILLION** tiny holes.

They contain acid that helps to dissolve your food.

It's the acid that makes your mouth and nose sting if you sick up your food.

Your two kidneys filter out waste water from your blood. This goes to your bladder where it stays until you pee.

Eyeball to eyeball

The pupil is a hole underneath the eye's outer coating. Light passes through it.

Your eyes take in pictures of what's around you, but they see everything upside down! Your brain turns them the right way up.

PUPIL

LENS

This coloured part of the eye is called the iris.

Our eyelids help to keep our eyes clean. They act a bit like car windscreen wipers when we blink.

If we get something in our eye, tears can help to wash it away.

Over the page, there are some great ways to trick your brain into seeing things that aren't there!

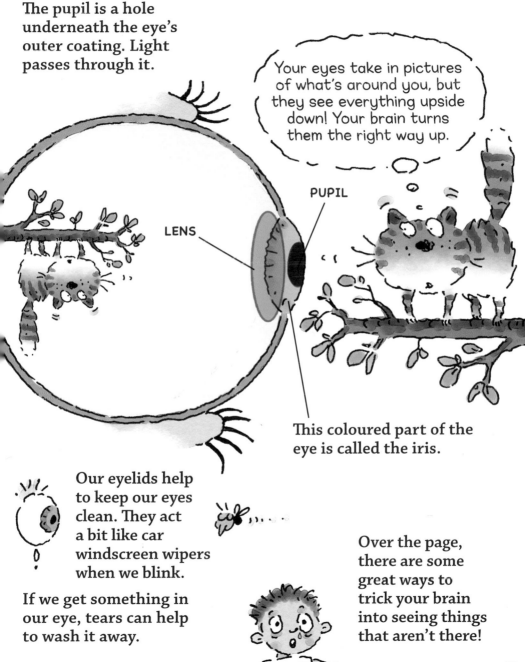

43

Don't believe your eyes!

When you look at this ring, it's obviously all one shade of grey.

Your brain keeps putting grey dots in the white circles, even though they're not there!

When you split the ring, it may look a little lighter on the left than on the right.

When you slide it down, the two halves look totally different shades of grey.

The first illusion is called Koffka's Ring. It's an example of our brain trying to make sense of what it sees and getting in a muddle!

This is weird, Jaggers!

???

44

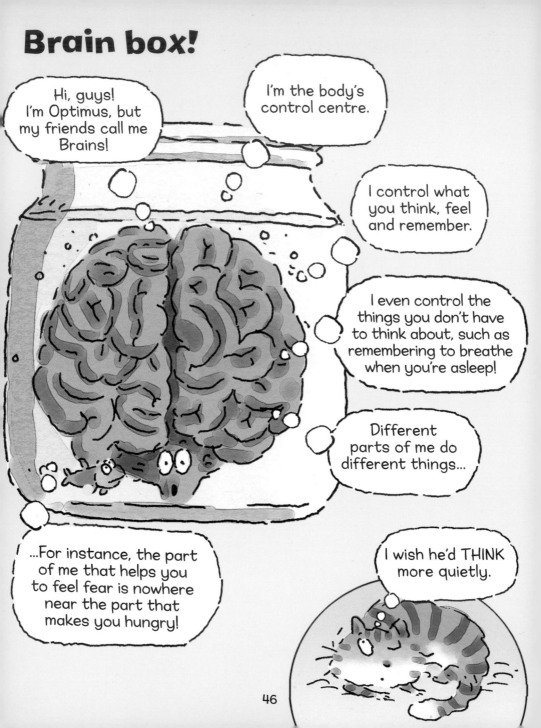

47

WHOA! What's happened to us, Jaggers?

It's nothing to worry about. The special lighting in this room shows u the nerves runnin all through our bodies, that's all.

WARNING!
BRAIN
IN JAR
THIS WAY

You've got nerve bringir us in here!

MESSAGE CARRIERS

Nerves pass messages to and from the brain. Nerve cells have three main jobs:

- to carry senses to the brain ("ouch!").
- to pass instructions from the brain to muscles (telling them what to do).
- to share information from the rest of the body.

MY BRILLIANT BRAIN
by Henry

There are BILLIONS of nerve cells in my brain.

They can receive around 100,000 messages a second.

These messages can be turned into my memories.

Messages can zip around at up to 270 miles an hour (435 kph)!

You can see a ball, catch it and throw it back in a few seconds, even though the messages making this happen have to pass through MILLIONS of nerve cells.

And, at the same time, I can think about all those slobbery DOGGY GERMS on the ball!

DRIBBLE!

DROOL!

49

The body fights back

How does our body fight germs, Jaggers?

Let's ask some in person! There are different types, you know... After you...

Hi, I'm William the Bacterium. Call me Bill. I love warm moist places and plenty of food, such as the human body!

You look harmless!

I am. Your body is full of friendly bacteria, but some harmful ones too.

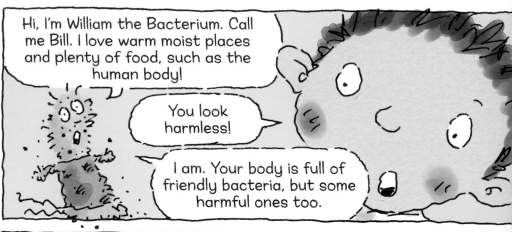

I'm Veronica the Virus. We invade your cells and force them into making more viruses!

That sounds a pretty mean trick, Veronica!

Not really, I'm just doing my job!

Leave me to die. You must fight on without me.

GOTCHA!

White blood cells wrap themselves around germs and break them into harmless pieces.

When you're ill, a high temperature is part of the battle to help you get well. The heat helps to kill germs.

It's hard work being a virus, you know. Your body is so good at fighting back!

Grow up!

Hi, Henry! I'm Wally Walnut from Room 404. My battle isn't with germs but with growing older ... and I reckon I'm WINNING!

I feel GREAT!

Eardrums losing their bounce, making it harder to hear.

Hair falling out. The hair that's left is turning white.

Teeth getting worn down.

Eyesight getting worse.

Skin wrinkling, because it has stretched over the years.

95 today

If you think I'm OLD, you should meet my DAD!

Bones getting thinner and weaker.

Blood vessels weakening.

Joints getting stiff.

Wally is in great shape for his age but, as we get older, our cells stop working so hard and fix themselves more slowly.

Fit 'n' healthy

Sweet dreams

Thanks for everything, Jaggers! It's been a COOL day! I think I could do with an early night.

No one knows for sure why we dream. Perhaps our brains are trying to make sense of the day.

We have dreams every night (even if we don't always remember them). Most of us have about 1,000 dreams a year!

57

The human body

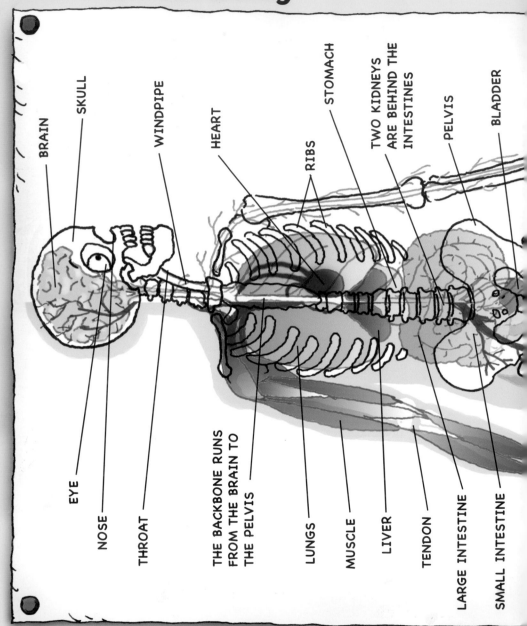

BRAIN

SKULL

WINDPIPE

HEART

STOMACH

TWO KIDNEYS
ARE BEHIND THE
INTESTINES

RIBS

PELVIS

BLADDER

EYE

NOSE

THROAT

THE BACKBONE RUNS
FROM THE BRAIN TO
THE PELVIS

LUNGS

MUSCLE

LIVER

TENDON

LARGE INTESTINE

SMALL INTESTINE

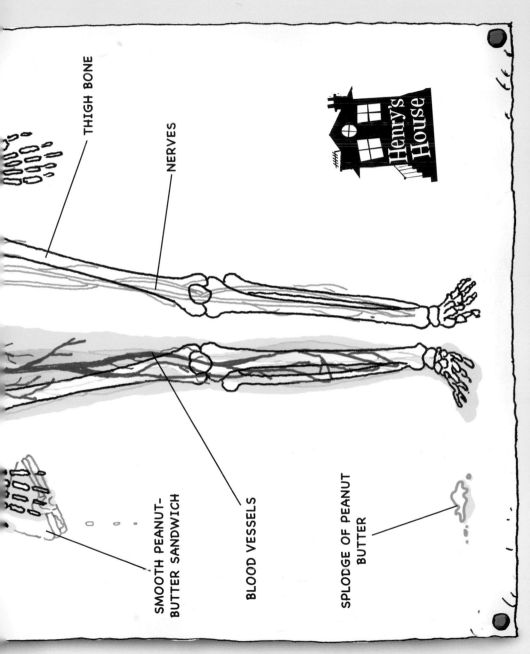

THIGH BONE

NERVES

Henry's House

SMOOTH PEANUT-
BUTTER SANDWICH

BLOOD VESSELS

SPLODGE OF PEANUT
BUTTER

Glossary

Acid: inside your stomach, this is a very strong liquid that helps to break down your food.

Allergic: caused by an allergy. An allergy is something which can make you unwell. It might make you sneeze, your eyes itch or even make you come out in spots.

Blood vessels: the narrow tubes in your body which your blood flows through.

Ear canal: the tube joining the outer part of your ear to the middle part.

Earwax: yellowish, sticky stuff that guards the ear canal from things getting down it.

Enamel: the hard, white surface of your teeth.

Filter: a way of separating the bits you want from something from the bits you don't!

Glands: make important juices that your body needs to work properly.

Mucus: sticky and slippery stuff in your nose and windpipe. It catches dust and bacteria, stopping them getting into your body.

Nerves: thin strands – imagine really thin wires – passing instructions and information to and from your brain telling you how to move and feel.

Nostrils: the two holes at the bottom of your nose that allow air and smells in and out.

Sensors: parts of your body which tell your brain when you touch or feel something, including heat.

3-D (three-dimensional): Something that has three dimensions; height, width and depth, rather than being flat like a drawing.

Index

Henry's House

We hope you enjoyed your visit

to **Henry's House**

Come back soon!

Look out for:
- **Creepy-crawlies**
- **Egyptians**
- **Dinosaurs**
- **Knights and Castles**
- **Space**